I0759120

How Many Btu Required To Cool 800 Ft2: The Simple Guide How Many Btu Required To Cool 800 Ft2

Joseph Robert

Published by CEBE Publishers, 2024.

While every precaution has been taken in the preparation of this book, the publisher assumes no responsibility for errors or omissions, or for damages resulting from the use of the information contained herein.

HOW MANY BTU REQUIRED TO COOL 800 FT2: THE SIMPLE GUIDE HOW MANY BTU REQUIRED TO COOL 800 FT2

First edition. February 8, 2024.

Copyright © 2024 Joseph Robert.

Written by Joseph Robert.

Table of Contents

How Many Btu Required To Cool 800 Ft2

The Simple Guide How Many Btu Required To Cool 800 Ft2

Joseph Robert

Disclaimer

While every precaution has been taken in the preparation of this book, the publisher assumes no responsibility for errors or omissions, or for damages resulting from the use of the information contained herein.

How Many Btu Required To Cool 800 Ft2: The Simple Guide How Many Btu Required To Cool 800 Ft2

First edition.

Copyright © Joseph Robert 2024. All Rights Reserved

Before this document can be legally duplicated or reproduced in any manner, the publisher's consent must be gained. Therefore, the contents within this document can neither be stored electronically, transferred, nor kept in a database. Neither in part, nor in full can this document be copied, scanned, faxed, or retained without approval from the publisher or creator.

Foreword

In the ever-evolving landscape of home comfort and energy efficiency, understanding the fundamental principles of cooling is paramount. "How Many BTU Required to Cool 800 ft²" serves as a beacon in the realm of practical knowledge, guiding readers through the intricacies of determining the ideal thermal solution for their living spaces.

As an experienced professional in the field, I commend the author's meticulous approach to unraveling the complexities of BTU calculations. This book not only demystifies the science behind cooling requirements but also empowers homeowners, architects, and HVAC professionals with invaluable insights.

The author's ability to distill technical information into accessible and actionable advice is commendable. Whether you're embarking on a home renovation project or seeking to optimize your existing cooling system, the knowledge within these pages will undoubtedly prove indispensable. From comprehensive explanations of heat gain factors to practical tips for selecting the right cooling capacity, this book is a comprehensive guide that transcends the boundaries of traditional HVAC literature.

In an era where sustainable living and energy-conscious choices are at the forefront, "How Many BTU Required to Cool 800 ft²" emerges as a timely and indispensable resource. It is my pleasure to endorse this work, confident that it will empower readers to make informed decisions, enhancing both their comfort and the efficiency of their living spaces.

Introduction

The Importance of Proper Cooling

The Importance of Proper Cooling: Enhancing Comfort and Efficiency:

In the ever-changing landscapes of home design and energy management, the significance of proper cooling cannot be overstated. This comprehensive exploration delves into the intricacies of maintaining optimal temperature in living spaces, underscoring the crucial balance between comfort and efficiency.

I. Unveiling the Foundations of Home Comfort

A. The Science Behind Thermal Comfort

- Defining the Basics: Temperature, Humidity, and Airflow

- Understanding the Human Element: Factors Influencing Comfort

B. The Role of Proper Cooling in Daily Living

- Enhancing Productivity and Well-Being

- Sleep Quality and Its Connection to Temperature Regulation

II. Navigating the Path to Energy Efficiency

A. Sustainable Cooling Practices

- Eco-Friendly Cooling Technologies

- The Intersection of Energy Conservation and Comfort

B. Financial Implications of Energy-Efficient Cooling

- Long-Term Cost Savings through Smart Cooling Choices

- Government Incentives and Rebates for Energy-Efficient Systems

III. Unpacking the BTU Dilemma: Sizing and Selection

A. Demystifying BTU (British Thermal Unit)

- A Practical Guide to Understanding BTU in Cooling Systems

- The Relationship Between BTU and Square Footage

B. Right-Sizing Cooling Systems for Optimal Performance

- Calculating BTU Requirements for Different Spaces

- Overcoming Common Challenges in System Selection

IV. Weathering the Seasons: Adaptive Cooling Strategies

A. Seasonal Considerations in Cooling

- Tailoring Cooling Solutions for Summer and Winter

- Year-Round Comfort: The Art of Efficient Climate Control

This exploration into the importance of proper cooling serves as a comprehensive guide, offering readers a wealth of practical knowledge to navigate the intricacies of maintaining a comfortable and energy-efficient living environment. Whether you're a homeowner, a designer, or an HVAC professional, the insights within these pages are designed to empower you on your journey to enhanced comfort and efficiency.

Energy Efficiency in Residential Spaces

Energy Efficiency in Residential Spaces: A Comprehensive Guide to Sustainable Living:

In our fast-paced world, the pursuit of energy efficiency in our homes has become a cornerstone of responsible living. This extensive exploration delves into the intricate landscape of residential energy efficiency, unraveling practical strategies and insightful considerations for homeowners seeking to reduce their environmental footprint and utility bills.

I. Navigating the Landscape of Residential Energy Efficiency

A. Understanding the Basics

- Defining Energy Efficiency in the Context of Homes

- The Economic and Environmental Imperatives

B. The Role of Residential Energy Efficiency in Climate Change Mitigation

- Global Perspectives on Household Energy Consumption

- The Power of Individual Actions in a Collective Effort

II. The Building Blocks of an Energy-Efficient Home

A. Insulation and Thermal Comfort

- Types of Insulation: A Comparative Analysis

- The Synergy Between Insulation and HVAC Systems

B. Efficient Lighting Solutions

- LED Technology: Illuminating the Path to Savings

- Practical Tips for Optimizing Lighting Efficiency

III. Smart Home Integration: The Future of Efficient Living

A. The Internet of Things (IoT) in Home Automation

- Connecting Devices for Seamless Energy Management

- Realizing the Potential of Smart Thermostats and Appliances

B. Energy Monitoring and Control Systems

- Empowering Homeowners with Real-Time Consumption Data

- Making Informed Decisions Through Smart Analytics

IV. Sustainable Energy Sources for Residential Spaces

This comprehensive guide to energy efficiency in residential spaces aims to equip readers with the knowledge and tools necessary to transform their homes into models of sustainable living. Whether you're a seasoned environmental advocate or just beginning your journey towards energy-conscious living, the insights within these pages are crafted to resonate with individuals of all backgrounds, providing a roadmap towards a more sustainable and efficient future.

Chapter 1

Understanding BTU Basics

Defining BTU (British Thermal Unit)

Defining BTU (British Thermal Unit): The Foundation of Efficient Heating and Cooling:

In the intricate world of thermal engineering, the term "BTU" stands as a fundamental unit that shapes the way we understand and measure heat. This comprehensive exploration aims to demystify the concept of BTU, shedding light on its significance in the context of heating, cooling, and energy efficiency.

I. Unveiling the Basics of BTU

A. Origin and Evolution of the British Thermal Unit

- Tracing the Historical Development of BTU Measurement

- The Adoption of BTU in Various Scientific Disciplines

B. The BTU in Everyday Terms

- Translating BTU into Practical Language

- Understanding Heat Energy through Everyday Examples

II. The Science Behind BTU Measurement

A. BTU as a Unit of Energy

- Clarifying BTU's Role in Measuring Heat Energy

- Relationship Between BTU and Other Units in Thermodynamics

B. Heat Transfer and BTU

- Conduction, Convection, and Radiation: Exploring Heat Transfer Mechanisms

- Quantifying Heat Exchange in BTU

III. Practical Applications of BTU in Heating Systems

A. Sizing Heating Systems: Matching BTU to Space

- Determining BTU Requirements for Efficient Heating

- Factors Influencing Heat Load Calculation

B. Efficient Distribution of Heat

- The Role of HVAC Systems in BTU Distribution

- Zoning and Its Impact on BTU Management in Buildings

IV. BTU in the Context of Cooling Systems

A. Understanding Cooling Capacity

This exploration into the world of BTU seeks to empower readers with a nuanced understanding of this critical unit of measurement. Whether you're a homeowner aiming to optimize your heating and cooling systems or an industry professional looking to enhance energy efficiency, the insights within these pages will serve as a valuable resource for navigating the complexities of BTU in the realm of thermal sciences.

Role of BTU in Cooling Systems

The Role of BTU in Cooling Systems: Navigating the Dynamics of Comfort:

In the intricate dance of thermal comfort, the British Thermal Unit (BTU) takes center stage, orchestrating the equilibrium between heat and coolness. This comprehensive exploration is a deep dive into the pivotal role that BTU plays in the realm of cooling systems, unraveling the complexities to empower homeowners and professionals alike.

I. Unveiling the Essence of BTU in Cooling

A. Defining BTU in the Context of Cooling

- Tracing the Roots of BTU Measurement in Cooling Technologies

- Understanding BTU as the Currency of Thermal Comfort

B. The Dynamics of Heat Removal

- How Cooling Systems Harness and Expel Heat

- The Relationship Between BTU and Cooling Capacity

II. Sizing Cooling Systems: A BTU Odyssey

A. Calculating Cooling Requirements

- Factors Influencing BTU Needs in Different Spaces

- The Science of Matching BTU to Square Footage

B. The Impact of Insulation on BTU Dynamics

- Insulation's Crucial Role in BTU Management

- Strategies for Optimizing Insulation for Efficient Cooling

III. Air Conditioners and BTU: The Perfect Synergy

A. Decoding Air Conditioner Specifications

- Understanding BTU Ratings on Air Conditioning Units

- The Pitfalls of Undersized or Oversized Systems

B. Zoning and BTU Distribution

- Achieving Precision through Zoned Cooling

- Maximizing BTU Efficiency in Different Areas of a Building

IV. Beyond Comfort: The Environmental Implications

A. Energy Efficiency and BTU Optimization

- The Quest for Sustainable Cooling Solutions

This journey through the role of BTU in cooling systems is crafted to enlighten and empower. Whether you're a homeowner seeking to optimize your cooling efficiency or an HVAC professional navigating the nuances of BTU management, the insights within these pages aim to provide clarity, foster awareness, and empower you to make informed decisions in the pursuit of cool, comfortable living.

Chapter 2

Calculating Heat Gain

Factors Influencing Heat Gain

Factors Influencing Heat Gain: Mastering the Art of Temperature Control

In the intricate ballet of maintaining indoor comfort, understanding the myriad factors influencing heat gain is paramount. This in-depth exploration navigates through the complexities of heat gain in residential and commercial spaces, providing a comprehensive guide for homeowners, architects, and HVAC professionals alike.

I. Unveiling the Foundations of Heat Gain

A. Solar Radiation and Its Impact

- The Sun as a Primary Heat Source: A Radiant Energy Overview

- Solar Angles and Their Seasonal Influence on Heat Intensity

B. The Role of Building Materials

- Conductive and Radiant Properties of Common Construction Materials

- Selecting Materials to Mitigate Heat Gain in Different Climates

II. Architectural Considerations in Heat Gain

A. Orientation and Building Layout

- Harnessing or Shielding from Solar Exposure: Design Principles

- Optimizing Building Orientation for Seasonal Comfort

B. Window Efficiency and Placement

- The Window Conundrum: Balancing Natural Light and Heat Gain

- Energy-Efficient Glazing Options for Managing Solar Heat Influx

III. Insulation: A Shield Against Unwanted Heat

A. Types of Insulation and Their Efficacy

- Batt, Spray Foam, and Reflective: Understanding the Insulation Toolbox

- Calculating Insulation R-Values for Optimal Heat Resistance

B. Roofing Strategies for Heat Gain Control

- Cool Roofs and Green Roofs: Strategies to Reflect or Absorb Solar Heat

- Ventilation Techniques for Attic Spaces to Prevent Heat Accumulation

IV. Appliances and Heat-Generating Equipment

A. The Impact of Electronic Devices

- Quantifying Heat Emissions from Common Appliances

XI. Frequently Asked Questions: Clarifying Common Inquiries

A. Expert Responses to Heat Gain Queries

- Addressing Concerns and Misconceptions Surrounding Heat Gain

- Practical Tips for Individuals Seeking Personalized Solutions

XII. Resources and References: A Knowledge Compendium

A. Additional Reading and References

- Recommended Books, Articles, and Online Resources

- Tools for Heat Gain Calculations and Analysis

XIII. Conclusion: Empowering Readers for Informed Heat Management

A. Recap of Key Insights

- Summarizing Essential Strategies for Heat Gain Control

- Inspiring Proactive Approaches to Achieve Optimal Thermal Comfort

This comprehensive guide to factors influencing heat gain is tailored to empower individuals with a holistic understanding of how to masterfully control indoor temperatures. Whether you're a homeowner seeking comfort or a professional striving for energy efficiency, the insights within these pages are crafted to guide you through the intricate dance of managing heat gain in the pursuit of ideal living and working environments.

Estimating Heat Gain in 800 ft² Spaces

Estimating Heat Gain in 800 ft² Spaces: A Practical Guide to Precision Cooling:

In the quest for optimal indoor comfort, understanding and estimating heat gain is a pivotal skill. This comprehensive exploration delves into the intricacies of heat gain in 800 ft² spaces, offering practical insights for homeowners, designers, and HVAC professionals to navigate the nuanced art of climate control.

I. Grasping the Basics of Heat Gain

A. Defining Heat Gain in Residential Settings

- Unraveling the Concept of Heat Gain: A Fundamental Overview

- The Interplay of Heat Sources and Temperature Dynamics

B. The Importance of Accurate Estimations

- Why Precision Matters: Implications of Underestimating or Overestimating Heat Gain

- Striking the Right Balance for Comfort and Energy Efficiency

II. Identifying Key Heat Sources in 800 ft² Spaces

A. Solar Heat Gain Through Windows

- Calculating Solar Heat Gain Coefficient (SHGC) for Different Window Types

- Strategies for Mitigating Solar Heat Influx in Compact Spaces

B. Appliances and Electronic Devices

- Quantifying Heat Emissions from Common Household Devices

- Efficient Placement and Usage for Minimizing Internal Heat Load

III. Understanding Internal Heat Generation

A. Human Activity and Occupancy

- Estimating Heat Emission from Occupants in 800 ft² Spaces

- Design Considerations for Improving Air Circulation and Comfort

B. Cooking and Kitchen Heat

- Analyzing Heat Gain During Culinary Activities

- Ventilation Solutions for Effective Heat Removal in Compact Kitchens

X. Resources and References: A Knowledge Compendium

A. Additional Reading and References

- Recommended Books, Articles, and Online Resources for Deeper Understanding

- Tools for Heat Gain Calculations and Analysis

XI. Conclusion: Equipping Readers for Informed Heat Gain Management

A. Summarizing Key Insights

- Providing Practical Takeaways for Efficient Heat Gain Control

- Inspiring Proactive Approaches to Achieve Optimal Indoor Climate

This comprehensive guide to estimating heat gain in 800 ft^2 spaces aims to empower readers with the knowledge and tools necessary for precision cooling. Whether you're a homeowner looking to enhance comfort or a professional seeking efficient HVAC solutions, the insights within these pages are designed to guide you through the intricacies of heat gain estimation and management for a more comfortable and energy-efficient living space.

Chapter 3

Determining Cooling Requirements

Matching BTU to Square Footage

Matching BTU to Square Footage: Precision in Temperature Control

Achieving the perfect balance between comfort and energy efficiency in your living space hinges on a fundamental principle: matching BTU (British Thermal Unit) to square footage. In this comprehensive exploration, we delve into the intricacies of this critical aspect of HVAC (Heating, Ventilation, and Air Conditioning) design, providing invaluable insights for homeowners, architects, and HVAC professionals.

I. Understanding the BTU Basics

A. Decoding BTU in Temperature Control

- Unveiling the Significance of BTU in Heating and Cooling Systems

- The Role of BTU in Quantifying Thermal Energy

B. Why Precision Matters

- Implications of Undersized or Oversized Systems

- Balancing Comfort, Efficiency, and Cost

II. Sizing Heating Systems: A BTU Odyssey

A. Calculating BTU Requirements for Winter Comfort

- Factors Influencing BTU Needs in Different Spaces

- The Impact of Local Climate on Sizing Decisions

B. Insulation's Crucial Role

- Insulation as a Key Factor in BTU Calculation

- Strategies for Optimizing Insulation for Efficient Heating

III. Cooling Considerations: BTU in Summertime

A. Matching BTU to Square Footage for Optimal Cooling

- Sizing Air Conditioners According to BTU Requirements

- The Seasonal Dynamics of Cooling Needs

B. Window Efficiency and Placement

- The Window Conundrum: Balancing Natural Light and Heat Gain

- Energy-Efficient Glazing Options for Managing Solar Heat Influx

IV. The Science of BTU Calculation

A. Demystifying BTU Calculations

HOW MANY BTU REQUIRED TO COOL 800 FT2

- Recommended Books, Articles, and Online Resources for Deeper Understanding

- Tools for BTU Calculations and Analysis

XI. Conclusion: Empowering Readers for Informed Sizing Choices

A. Summarizing Key Insights

- Providing Practical Takeaways for Efficient BTU Matching

- Inspiring Proactive Approaches to Achieve Optimal Indoor Climate

This thorough exploration into matching BTU to square footage is crafted to enlighten and empower. Whether you're a homeowner looking to optimize your HVAC system or a professional navigating the complexities of sizing for diverse spaces, the insights within these pages aim to provide clarity, foster awareness, and empower you to make informed decisions in the pursuit of ideal heating and cooling solutions for any space.

Adjusting for Insulation and Climate

Adjusting for Insulation and Climate: Mastering Temperature Control:

In the pursuit of optimal comfort and energy efficiency, the dynamics of adjusting for insulation and climate play a pivotal role. This in-depth exploration aims to unravel the intricacies of how insulation and climate considerations intersect, offering invaluable insights for homeowners, architects, and HVAC professionals seeking to navigate the nuanced landscape of temperature control.

I. Understanding the Essence of Insulation

A. The Role of Insulation in Temperature Regulation

- Unveiling the Significance of Insulation in Residential and Commercial Spaces

- Types of Insulation: From Fiberglass to Foam, Decoding the Options

B. The Science Behind Heat Transfer

- Conductive, Convective, and Radiant Heat: How Insulation Battles Each

- Calculating Insulation R-Values: A Guide to Thermal Resistance

II. Tailoring Insulation to Different Climates

A. Insulation Strategies for Cold Climates

- Battling Winter Chill: Optimizing Insulation for Heat Retention

- The Impact of Snow and Ice on Roofing and Insulation Performance

B. Cooling Solutions for Hotter Regions

- Heat Resilience: Insulation Practices for Managing High Temperatures

- Addressing Humidity Challenges Through Insulation Techniques

III. Climatic Factors Influencing Temperature Control

A. Understanding the Impact of Local Climate

- The Microclimate Challenge: Navigating Temperature Variations in Regions

- The Role of Wind, Sun Exposure, and Precipitation in Climate-Responsive Design

B. Seasonal Adjustments for Temperature Comfort

This comprehensive guide to adjusting for insulation and climate is crafted to enlighten and empower. Whether you're a homeowner looking to optimize temperature control or a professional striving for energy-efficient building practices, the insights within these pages aim to provide clarity, foster awareness, and empower you to make informed decisions in the pursuit of ideal insulation and climate-adaptive solutions.

Chapter 4

Choosing the Right Cooling System

Overview of Cooling Options

Overview of Cooling Options: Navigating the Chill:

In the realm of temperature control, the array of cooling options available can be as diverse as the climates they serve. This comprehensive exploration delves into the world of cooling technologies, offering insights into various methods, innovations, and considerations. Whether you're a homeowner looking for the best solution or a professional in the HVAC industry, this guide aims to equip you with the knowledge needed to make informed decisions for optimal cooling.

I. Introduction to Cooling Technologies

A. Understanding the Fundamentals

- The Essence of Cooling in Residential and Commercial Environments

- Core Principles: Heat Exchange, Refrigeration, and Thermodynamics

B. Types of Cooling Systems

- Air Conditioning: Central, Split, Window, and Ductless Options

- Evaporative Cooling: Harnessing the Power of Water for Temperature Control

- Geothermal Cooling: Tapping into Earth's Constant Temperature for Efficiency

II. Sizing Up the Space: Choosing the Right Cooling Capacity

A. Calculating BTU Requirements

- The Role of British Thermal Units (BTU) in Sizing Cooling Systems

- Matching Cooling Capacity to Square Footage: Avoiding Overcooling or Undercooling

B. Factors Influencing Sizing Decisions

- Insulation, Windows, and Climate: Key Variables in Determining Cooling Needs

- Customizing Solutions Based on Room Function and Usage Patterns

III. Energy-Efficient Cooling Solutions

A. The Quest for Sustainability

- High-Efficiency HVAC Systems: SEER Ratings and Energy Savings

HOW MANY BTU REQUIRED TO COOL 800 FT2

This comprehensive guide to cooling options is crafted to enlighten and empower. Whether you're a homeowner seeking comfort or a professional navigating the complexities of cooling technology, the insights within these pages aim to provide clarity, foster awareness, and empower you to make informed decisions in the pursuit of optimal cooling solutions for any space.

Sizing Air Conditioners for Optimal Performance

Sizing Air Conditioners for Optimal Performance: The Art of Precision Cooling:

In the ever-evolving landscape of climate control, the proper sizing of air conditioners emerges as a linchpin for achieving not only comfort but also efficiency and cost-effectiveness. This comprehensive guide delves into the intricacies of sizing air conditioners, providing insights for homeowners, HVAC professionals, and anyone seeking mastery in the quest for optimal cooling.

I. Understanding the Importance of Proper Sizing

A. The Impact of Undersized Systems

- Unveiling the Consequences of Insufficient Cooling Capacity

- Striking the Balance: Avoiding the Pitfalls of Under dimensioned Air Conditioning

B. The Dangers of Oversizing

- Overcoming the Myths Surrounding Bigger-Is-Better Mentality

- Energy Waste and Comfort Compromises: The Downsides of Oversized AC Units

II. The Science Behind BTU (British Thermal Unit)

A. Decoding BTU in Air Conditioning

- BTU as the Standard Unit for Cooling Power

- Calculating Cooling Needs Based on BTU Requirements

B. Factors Influencing BTU Calculation

- Square Footage, Insulation, and Climate: Variables in Determining BTU Needs

- Customizing BTU Requirements for Different Rooms and Spaces

III. Calculating the Right Size for Different Spaces

A. Residential Air Conditioning Sizing Strategies

- Bedrooms, Living Rooms, and Kitchens: Tailoring Cooling Capacity

- Zoning Approaches for Enhanced Comfort and Energy Efficiency

HOW MANY BTU REQUIRED TO COOL 800 FT2

- Inspiring Proactive Approaches to Achieve Ideal Indoor Comfort Through Precision Cooling

This comprehensive guide to sizing air conditioners is crafted to enlighten and empower. Whether you're a homeowner seeking comfort or an HVAC professional navigating the complexities of cooling technology, the insights within these pages aim to provide clarity, foster awareness, and empower you to make informed decisions in the pursuit of optimal cooling solutions for any space.

Chapter 5

Practical Considerations

Maintenance Tips for Efficient Cooling

Maintenance Tips for Efficient Cooling: Prolonging the Chill:

In the pursuit of a consistently cool and comfortable indoor environment, the key lies not only in the initial installation of a cooling system but in the diligent maintenance that follows. This comprehensive guide explores essential maintenance tips designed to enhance the efficiency, lifespan, and overall performance of cooling systems. Whether you're a homeowner looking to optimize your air conditioner or an HVAC professional seeking best practices, these insights aim to empower you with the knowledge needed to keep the cool breeze flowing seamlessly.

I. Introduction to Cooling System Maintenance

A. The Significance of Regular Maintenance

- Understanding the Relationship Between Maintenance and Efficiency

- Prolonging the Lifespan of Cooling Systems Through Diligent Care

B. Common Maintenance Misconceptions

- Debunking Myths Surrounding Cooling System Care

- Dispelling Notions That Could Compromise System Efficiency

II. The Importance of Regular Filter Changes

A. Role of Air Filters in Cooling Systems

- Trapping Dust, Pollen, and Allergens: The Crucial Function of Filters

- Consequences of Clogged Filters on System Efficiency and Air Quality

B. Frequency and Methods of Filter Replacement

- Customizing Replacement Schedules Based on System Type and Usage

- Step-by-Step Guide to Properly Changing Air Filters for Optimal Performance

III. Cleaning and Maintaining Evaporator and Condenser Coils

A. Understanding Coil Functions

- Heat Absorption and Release: The Coordinated Dance of Evaporator and Condenser Coils

- The Impact of Dirty Coils on System Efficiency and Cooling Capacity

B. Best Practices in Coil Cleaning

Smart Thermostats and Energy Management

Smart Thermostats and Energy Management: Mastering Comfort with Precision and Efficiency

In the realm of modern home comfort, the marriage of technology and energy management has given rise to a revolutionary tool—the smart thermostat. This comprehensive exploration delves into the intricacies of smart thermostats, unraveling their potential to not only control temperatures but to optimize energy consumption. Whether you're a homeowner looking to upgrade or an enthusiast intrigued by the future of climate control, this guide aims to unravel the intelligence behind smart thermostats and their pivotal role in reshaping how we manage energy in our living spaces.

I. Introduction to Smart Thermostats: Beyond Temperature Control

A. The Evolution of Home Climate Control

- From Manual Thermostats to Smart, Connected Solutions

- Unveiling the Technological Advancements Driving the Smart Thermostat Revolution

B. Defining Smart Thermostats

- Characteristics and Features That Define Smart Thermostats

- How They Differ From Traditional Thermostats in Functionality and Capability

II. The Technological Core: How Smart Thermostats Work

A. Sensors and Data Analytics

- The Importance of Accurate Data for Smart Decision-Making

- Understanding the Array of Sensors Packed Into Smart Thermostats

B. Connectivity: Wi-Fi and Beyond

- Remote Access and Control: The Role of Wi-Fi Connectivity

- Integration with Smart Home Ecosystems and Voice-Activated Assistants

III. The Intelligent Brain: Algorithms and Learning Capabilities

A. Adaptive Learning

- How Smart Thermostats Learn Your Habits and Preferences

- The Role of Machine Learning Algorithms in Adaptive Climate Control

- Exploring Advanced Features and Customization Options Through User Manuals and Guides

XIII. Conclusion: Empowering Homes for a Smart Climate Future

A. Reflecting on the Journey

- Unveiling the Transformative Power of Smart Thermostats in Home Climate Control

- Inspiring Proactive Approaches to Achieve Ideal Indoor Comfort Through Precision Energy Management

This guide stands as a beacon for those venturing into the realm of smart thermostats and energy management, guiding them through the intricate landscape of technology, efficiency, and personalized comfort. May it illuminate the path towards a future where homes are not just spaces of shelter, but intelligent environments that adapt seamlessly to the needs and preferences of those who inhabit them.

Chapter 6

Case Studies

Real-Life Examples of BTU Calculations

Real-Life Examples of BTU Calculations: Unveiling the Science Behind Comfort

In the intricate dance of heating, ventilation, and air conditioning (HVAC) systems, the concept of British Thermal Units (BTUs) takes center stage. For homeowners, architects, and HVAC professionals alike, understanding how to calculate the appropriate BTU capacity for a space is essential to achieving optimal comfort. In this exploration, we delve into real-life examples of BTU calculations, demystifying the process and showcasing its practical applications in diverse settings. From cozy living rooms to expansive commercial spaces, these examples illuminate the importance of precision in determining the right amount of thermal energy needed for a space to reach its ideal temperature.

I. Introduction to BTU Calculations: The Heartbeat of HVAC Efficiency

A. The Fundamental Role of BTUs in HVAC

- Grasping the Essence of British Thermal Units in Heating and Cooling

- How Accurate BTU Calculations Translate to Energy-Efficient Comfort

B. The Impact of Incorrect BTU Sizing

- Consequences of Undersized or Oversized Systems on Comfort and Efficiency

- Real-Life Scenarios Highlighting the Ramifications of Miscalculated BTUs

II. BTU Calculation Basics: A Step-by-Step Guide

A. Understanding the Factors Influencing BTU Requirements

- Square Footage, Insulation, and Climate: Key Variables in the Equation

- Determining Specific Heating and Cooling Needs Based on Space Characteristics

B. The Formula Unveiled

- Breaking Down the BTU Calculation Formula for Heating and Cooling

- Real-Life Examples Applying the Formula to Different Spaces and Environments

III. Residential BTU Calculations: Tailoring Comfort to Home Spaces

Success Stories in Efficient Cooling Solutions

Success Stories in Efficient Cooling Solutions: Transforming Spaces with Innovation and Sustainability

In the ever-evolving landscape of climate control, success stories emerge as beacons of inspiration, showcasing the transformative power of efficient cooling solutions. From residential homes to large commercial complexes, these narratives illustrate how innovative technologies, thoughtful design, and sustainability principles converge to create environments that not only beat the heat but do so with a mindful eye on energy efficiency. Join us on a journey through these success stories, each a testament to the triumphs of ingenuity and a commitment to creating cool, comfortable, and eco-friendly spaces.

I. Introduction: The Pinnacle of Cool Comfort

A. Defining Efficient Cooling

- Unveiling the Criteria for Success in Cooling Solutions

- The Intersection of Comfort, Innovation, and Sustainability

B. The Importance of Success Stories

- Drawing Inspiration from Real-Life Examples

- How Success Stories Shape the Future of Cooling Technologies

II. Residential Marvels: Cooling Homes with Precision

A. Net-Zero Homes: The Ultimate in Sustainable Cooling

- Success Stories of Homes Generating as Much Energy as They Consume

- Innovative Cooling Strategies in Net-Zero Home Design

B. Smart Homes Redefining Comfort

- Integration of Smart Technologies for Energy-Efficient Cooling

- Case Studies Showcasing Intelligent Cooling Solutions in Modern Residences

C. Historic Homes, Modern Cooling

- Success Stories of Retrofitting Historic Homes for Energy-Efficient Cooling

- Balancing Preservation with Innovation in Cooling Upgrades

III. Commercial Wonders: Symbiosis of Cooling and Sustainability

JOSEPH ROBERT

A. Additional Reading and References

- Recommended Books, Articles,

Chapter 7

Future Trends in Cooling Technology

Innovations Shaping the Future of Residential Cooling

Innovations Shaping the Future of Residential Cooling: A Glimpse into Tomorrow's Cool Homes

As technology continues to evolve, so does the landscape of residential cooling. From energy-efficient systems to smart home integration, the future of keeping our homes cool is undergoing a revolution. This exploration into the innovations shaping the future of residential cooling unveils the latest trends, cutting-edge technologies, and sustainable practices that promise not only a comfortable home environment but also a greener and more efficient future.

I. Introduction: The Evolving Face of Residential Cooling

A. Defining the Future of Residential Cooling

- Unveiling the Dynamics of Technological Advancements

- The Interplay Between Comfort, Efficiency, and Sustainability

B. Why Innovation Matters

- Addressing the Need for Progressive Cooling Solutions

- The Impact of Innovation on Energy Consumption and Environmental Footprint

II. Energy-Efficient HVAC Systems: Paving the Way for Sustainability

A. Next-Generation Air Conditioning Units

- The Rise of Variable Refrigerant Flow (VRF) Systems

- Success Stories of High-Efficiency Cooling Units in Residential Settings

B. Geothermal Heat Pumps: Harnessing Earth's Energy

- How Geothermal Systems Revolutionize Residential Cooling

- Case Studies of Geothermal Heat Pump Installations and Their Benefits

C. The Role of Insulation and Ventilation

- Innovations in Insulation Materials and Techniques

- Ventilation Strategies for Optimal Indoor Air Quality and Energy Savings

III. Smart Homes and Intelligent Cooling Solutions

A. Integration of Smart Thermostats

- The Impact of Smart Technology on Residential Cooling

B. Peak Load Management

- Strategies for Balancing Cooling Demand During Peak Hours

- Examples of Homes Effectively Managing Peak Cooling Loads

VIII. The Future of Personalized Cooling Comfort

A. Wearable Cooling Technologies

- Innovations in Wearable Devices for Personalized Climate Control

- How Wearable Tech Enhances the Residential Cooling Experience

B. Zoning and Customizable Cooling

- Residential Cooling Systems That Adapt to Individual Preferences

- Case Studies of Homes with Zoning Capabilities for Personalized Comfort

IX. Overcoming Challenges: Navigating Obstacles in Future Cooling

A. Affordability and Accessibility of Innovations

- Addressing Challenges in Making Cutting-Edge Cooling Technologies Accessible

- Strategies for Overcoming Economic Barriers to Adoption

B. Regulatory Considerations and Standards

- The Role of Regulations in Shaping the Future of Residential Cooling

- Successful Implementations in Compliance with Regulatory Standards

X. Future Collaborations: The Intersection of Residential Cooling and Urban Planning

A. Cooling Cities: Urban Planning for Sustainable Residential Climates

- How Urban Planners Consider Residential Cooling in City Designs

- Success Stories of Cities Implementing Residential Cooling Initiatives

XI. Lessons Learned and Looking Forward: Shaping a Cooler Future

A. Key Takeaways from Emerging Residential Cooling Innovations

- Common Themes Across Success Stories and Technological Advances

- Anticipating Continued Innovations in Residential Cooling

XII. Frequently Asked Questions: Expert Insights on Future Residential Cooling

A. Addressing Common Queries Surrounding Innovative Residential Cooling

- Practical Advice and Expert Opinions on the Future of Residential Cooling Technologies

- Tips for Homeowners Planning to Embrace Advanced Cooling Solutions

XIII. Resources and References: A Knowledge Compendium
A. Additional Reading and References
- Recommended Books, Articles, and Resources for Further Exploration

Sustainable Practices in HVAC

Sustainable Practices in HVAC: Pioneering a Green Revolution in Heating, Ventilation, and Air Conditioning

In the pursuit of environmental stewardship and energy efficiency, the HVAC (Heating, Ventilation, and Air Conditioning) industry is experiencing a paradigm shift towards sustainable practices. This comprehensive exploration delves into the key principles, innovations, and success stories that define the journey towards sustainable HVAC systems. From eco-friendly refrigerants to energy-efficient technologies, discover how the industry is reshaping the way we heat and cool our spaces while minimizing environmental impact.

I. Introduction: The Imperative for Sustainable HVAC Practices

A. Understanding the Environmental Impact of Traditional HVAC Systems

- The Carbon Footprint of Conventional HVAC Technologies

- The Ecological Consequences of High Energy Consumption in Heating and Cooling

B. The Urgency of Transitioning to Sustainable HVAC

- Global Climate Concerns and the Role of HVAC in Emission Reduction

- Why Sustainable Practices are Crucial for the Future of Comfortable Living

II. Eco-Friendly Refrigerants: A Critical Shift in Cooling Solutions

A. Phasing Out Harmful Refrigerants

- The Environmental Impact of Traditional Refrigerants (CFCs, HCFCs, HFCs)

- The Global Movement Towards Low-GWP (Global Warming Potential) Refrigerants

B. Natural Refrigerants: Harnessing Nature's Cooling Power

- Exploring Alternatives like Hydrocarbons, Ammonia, and Carbon Dioxide

- Success Stories of Implementing Natural Refrigerants in HVAC Systems

Chapter 8

Frequently Asked Questions

Common Queries Answered

Common Queries Answered: A Comprehensive Guide to Understanding HVAC Principles

In the realm of Heating, Ventilation, and Air Conditioning (HVAC), a myriad of questions arises as individuals seek optimal comfort and efficiency in their living and working spaces. This book aims to address these common queries, providing accurate and insightful information to demystify HVAC concepts. Whether you're a homeowner, a business owner, or simply curious about the world of HVAC, this guide covers essential topics to enhance your understanding and empower you to make informed decisions regarding your heating and cooling systems.

I. Introduction: Navigating the World of HVAC Questions

A. Setting the Stage: The Importance of Understanding HVAC Basics

- Why Knowledge about HVAC Matters for Comfort and Efficiency

- Dispelling Common Misconceptions in the HVAC Sphere

B. The Format of Common Queries Addressed in this Guide

- Categorizing Questions for Clarity and Easy Reference

- How This Guide Can Serve as a Go-To Resource for HVAC Information

II. Basics of HVAC: Answering Fundamental Questions

A. What is HVAC, and How Does it Work?

- Defining the Components of HVAC Systems

- The Interplay of Heating, Ventilation, and Air Conditioning in Maintaining Comfort

B. Why is Proper Ventilation Crucial?

- Understanding the Role of Ventilation in Indoor Air Quality

- How Ventilation Impacts Health and Comfort in Residential and Commercial Spaces

III. Selecting the Right HVAC System: Addressing Installation Queries

A. How Do I Choose the Right Size of HVAC System for My Space?

- The Importance of Proper Sizing in HVAC Installation

- Calculating BTU Requirements for Efficient Heating and Cooling

HOW MANY BTU REQUIRED TO COOL 800 FT2

Troubleshooting Cooling Challenges

Troubleshooting Cooling Challenges: A Comprehensive Guide to Resolving HVAC Issues

In the ever-evolving landscape of Heating, Ventilation, and Air Conditioning (HVAC), encountering cooling challenges is not uncommon. Whether you're a homeowner, a business owner, or an HVAC enthusiast, understanding how to troubleshoot cooling issues is crucial for maintaining optimal comfort and efficiency. This comprehensive guide delves into the intricacies of common cooling challenges, providing accurate information and actionable solutions to empower you in tackling HVAC issues with confidence.

Table of Contents

- The Importance of a Proactive Approach in Maintaining HVAC System Health

- Encouraging Ongoing Learning and Collaboration for HVAC Success

Chapter 9

Resources and References

Additional Reading and References

Additional Reading and References: Expanding Your Knowledge on HVAC and Cooling Systems

In the dynamic realm of Heating, Ventilation, and Air Conditioning (HVAC), staying abreast of the latest developments, research, and industry insights is paramount. This section serves as a curated collection of additional reading and references, providing enthusiasts, professionals, and curious minds with a roadmap to delve deeper into the multifaceted world of HVAC and cooling systems.

I. Foundational Literature

1. "Modern Refrigeration and Air Conditioning" by Andrew D. Althouse, Carl H. Turnquist, and Alfred F. Bracciano

This seminal work offers a comprehensive exploration of refrigeration and air conditioning principles. Readers will find in-depth discussions on fundamental concepts, system components, and troubleshooting techniques. The book caters to both novices and seasoned professionals, making it an invaluable resource for building a strong foundation in HVAC.

2. "ASHRAE Handbook – HVAC Systems and Equipment"

Published by the American Society of Heating, Refrigerating and Air-Conditioning Engineers (ASHRAE), this handbook is a treasure trove of information on HVAC systems and equipment. It covers a wide range of topics, including system selection, energy conservation, and sustainability. HVAC engineers, designers, and enthusiasts will discover authoritative insights to inform their practice.

II. Cutting-Edge Research Journals

1. "ASHRAE Journal"

The official publication of ASHRAE, the ASHRAE Journal, is a monthly magazine that covers a plethora of HVAC-related topics. From case studies and technical articles to discussions on emerging technologies, this journal provides a snapshot of the industry's latest trends and innovations. Regular perusal is recommended for professionals seeking to stay at the forefront of HVAC advancements.

2. "HVAC&R Research"

Dive into the world of research with "HVAC&R Research," a peer-reviewed journal that publishes scientific and technical papers. This journal is a vital resource for those interested in exploring cutting-edge research on topics like energy efficiency, indoor air quality, and sustainable HVAC solutions.

III. Specialized Publications

1. "Energy-Efficient HVAC Design: An Essential Guide for Sustainable Building" by Ljubomir Jankovic

For those passionate about sustainable HVAC practices, this book offers a detailed guide to designing energy-efficient HVAC systems. It explores strategies for minimizing environmental impact while maximizing energy savings, making it a must-read for architects, engineers, and environmentally conscious individuals.

2. "HVAC Water Chillers and Cooling Towers: Fundamentals, Application, and Operation" by Herbert W. Stanford III

Delve into the intricacies of water chillers and cooling towers with this comprehensive guide. The book covers fundamental principles, applications, and operational aspects, providing valuable insights for HVAC professionals involved in system design and maintenance.

IV. Online Resources

1. ASHRAE Learning Institute (ALI) Courses

Explore a variety of online courses offered by ALI, the educational arm of ASHRAE. From fundamentals to specialized topics, these courses cater to professionals seeking continuous education in HVAC. The interactive nature of the courses enhances learning and application.

2. HVAC School Podcast

For those who prefer auditory learning, the HVAC School Podcast covers a range of HVAC topics through insightful interviews and discussions. Hosted by industry expert Bryan Orr, the podcast offers practical knowledge and real-world experiences.

V. Research Institutions and Organizations

1. National Institute of Standards and Technology (NIST) – Building and Fire Research Laboratory

NIST conducts extensive research in the areas of building technology, fire research, and HVAC systems. Exploring their publications and research findings provides access to cutting-edge advancements in HVAC technology.

2. Air-Conditioning, Heating, and Refrigeration Institute (AHRI)

AHRI is a leading authority on HVACR performance and efficiency. Their publications and research initiatives contribute to industry standards and advancements. Professionals can benefit from staying informed about AHRI's latest publications and initiatives.

VI. Industry Conferences and Expositions

1. AHR Expo

The AHR Expo is a premier event in the HVAC industry, featuring the latest products, technologies, and innovations. Attending or following updates from such conferences provides firsthand exposure to emerging trends and fosters networking within the HVAC community.

2. ASHRAE Conferences

Participate in ASHRAE conferences, where experts and professionals gather to exchange knowledge and ideas. These conferences cover a wide range of HVAC-related topics and offer opportunities to engage with thought leaders in the field.

Conclusion

Expanding your knowledge in HVAC and cooling systems is an ongoing journey. The resources mentioned above provide a robust starting point for those eager to delve deeper into the intricacies of HVAC technology, sustainable practices, and industry advancements. Remember, the field is dynamic, and staying informed is key to achieving excellence in the ever-evolving world of heating, ventilation, and air conditioning.

Tools for BTU Calculations

Tools for BTU Calculations: A Comprehensive Guide

In the realm of heating, ventilation, and air conditioning (HVAC), accurate BTU (British Thermal Unit) calculations are the bedrock of efficient system design. Whether you're an HVAC professional, a homeowner, or someone with a keen interest in understanding the nuances of thermal comfort, having the right tools at your disposal is essential. This comprehensive guide explores the various tools used in BTU calculations, providing insights into their functionalities and applications.

I. Thermocouples and Thermistors

1. Overview:

Thermocouples and thermistors are temperature sensors crucial for BTU calculations. They measure the temperature difference across a system, allowing for accurate assessment.

2. Application:

Used in conjunction with airflow measurements, these sensors help determine the heat exchange rate, a critical factor in BTU calculations.

3. Popular Models:

- Type K Thermocouples

- Negative Temperature Coefficient (NTC) Thermistors

II. Psychrometers

1. Overview:

Psychrometers measure the moisture content in the air, a vital component for accurate BTU calculations as humidity influences thermal comfort.

2. Application:

Used to determine the enthalpy of the air, enabling precise calculations related to latent heat.

3. Popular Models:

- Digital Psychrometers with Multi-Functionality

III. Anemometers

1. Overview:

Anemometers measure airflow speed, an essential parameter when evaluating heat transfer rates.

2. Application:

Used to calculate the sensible heat in a space, aiding in BTU calculations for effective climate control.

3. Popular Models:

- Hot-Wire Anemometers

- Vane Anemometers

IV. Infrared Thermometers

1. Overview:

Infrared thermometers provide non-contact temperature measurements, useful for assessing surface temperatures in HVAC systems.

2. Application:

Used to identify temperature variations in components like radiators and coils, contributing to accurate BTU computations.

3. Popular Models:

- Spot Infrared Thermometers

- Infrared Thermometer Guns

V. Data Loggers

1. Overview:

Data loggers record temperature and humidity over time, offering a comprehensive dataset for BTU calculations.

2. Application:

Vital for understanding the dynamic nature of thermal conditions, especially in spaces with varying occupancy and usage patterns.

3. Popular Models:

- Wireless Data Loggers

- USB Data Loggers

VI. HVAC System Simulation Software

1. Overview:

Advanced HVAC simulation software models entire systems, facilitating intricate BTU calculations for complex environments.

2. Application:

HOW MANY BTU REQUIRED TO COOL 800 FT2

Ideal for professionals designing HVAC systems, allowing virtual experimentation before physical implementation.

3. Popular Software:

- EnergyPlus

- TRACE 3D Plus

VII. Online BTU Calculators

1. Overview:

Online BTU calculators simplify the process for homeowners and small businesses, offering quick estimations.

2. Application:

Practical for simple calculations, providing insights into potential heating and cooling requirements.

3. Popular Tools:

- BTU Calculator by Square Footage

- HVAC-Calc Residential Heat Loss & Heat Gain

Conclusion

As technology continues to evolve, so do the tools available for BTU calculations. Whether you're conducting a simple estimation or designing a sophisticated HVAC system, choosing the right tools is paramount. This guide serves as a roadmap, helping you navigate the diverse landscape of tools essential for precise and efficient BTU calculations. Stay informed, stay precise, and embrace the ever-expanding toolkit in the world of HVAC.

Recap of Key Takeaways

Recap of Key Takeaways: Unveiling the World of Efficient Cooling

As we conclude our exploration into the intricacies of efficient cooling, let's recap the key takeaways that empower you with a holistic understanding of this crucial aspect in residential spaces. From the foundational principles to advanced tools, our journey has been both enlightening and practical.

I. Importance of Proper Cooling

Understanding the fundamental importance of proper cooling lays the groundwork for creating comfortable and energy-efficient living spaces. From enhancing air quality to maintaining optimal temperatures, the benefits are manifold.

II. Energy Efficiency in Residential Spaces

Delving into the realm of energy efficiency unveils a spectrum of strategies, from smart thermostats to sustainable practices. Implementing these not only conserves energy but also contributes to environmental sustainability.

III. Defining BTU (British Thermal Unit)

The BTU, a cornerstone in our exploration, represents the heat needed to raise the temperature of one pound of water by one degree Fahrenheit. This unit is pivotal in sizing air conditioners and understanding the dynamics of cooling systems.

IV. Role of BTU in Cooling Systems

Matching the BTU to square footage is a nuanced process, requiring precision to ensure optimal performance. This match ensures that cooling systems can handle the heat load of a space efficiently.

V. Factors Influencing Heat Gain

Recognizing the factors influencing heat gain is crucial. From insulation to climate, each element contributes to the overall heat dynamics of a space. Adapting to these factors is key to effective cooling.

VI. Estimating Heat Gain in 800 ft² Spaces

In the context of 800 ft² spaces, estimating heat gain involves a meticulous calculation process. This knowledge is invaluable for homeowners seeking to enhance their cooling systems.

VII. Matching BTU to Square Footage

The formula for matching BTU to square footage is straightforward but requires attention to detail. This matching ensures that the cooling system is neither overpowered nor underpowered for a given space.

VIII. Adjusting for Insulation and Climate

Recognizing the impact of insulation and climate on cooling needs is a game-changer. This adjustment ensures that the cooling system is tailored to the specific conditions of a residence.

IX. Sizing Air Conditioners for Optimal Performance

Sizing air conditioners involves a delicate balance. An undersized unit struggles to cool adequately, while an oversized one leads to inefficiency. The right size ensures optimal performance.

X. Overview of Cooling Options

Our exploration into cooling options reveals a plethora of choices, from traditional air conditioners to innovative solutions. Each option has its merits, allowing homeowners to choose based on their unique requirements.

XI. Real-Life Examples of BTU Calculations

Real-life examples of BTU calculations offer practical insights into how this knowledge translates into effective decision-making. These scenarios provide a bridge between theory and application.

XII. Success Stories in Efficient Cooling Solutions

Success stories exemplify the positive impact of efficient cooling solutions. From residential homes to commercial spaces, these narratives inspire and motivate the pursuit of optimal comfort.

XIII. Innovations Shaping the Future of Residential Cooling

Looking ahead, innovations in residential cooling promise transformative changes. From smart thermostats to sustainable practices, the future is marked by technological advancements and eco-friendly solutions.

XIV. Sustainable Practices in HVAC

Embracing sustainable practices in HVAC aligns with the global shift towards environmentally conscious living. From energy-efficient systems to green building designs, sustainability is the guiding principle.

XV. Smart Thermostats and Energy Management

Smart thermostats and energy management systems redefine the way we interact with our indoor environments. These technologies empower homeowners to control and optimize their cooling systems intelligently.

XVI. Real-Life Examples of BTU Calculations

Our journey into real-life examples of BTU calculations reinforces the practicality of this knowledge. From residential spaces to commercial settings, the ability to calculate BTU is a valuable skill.

XVII. Troubleshooting Cooling Challenges

The troubleshooting of cooling challenges requires a systematic approach. Identifying and addressing issues promptly ensures the continuous and efficient operation of cooling systems.

XVIII. Additional Reading and References

Providing additional reading and references opens the door to further exploration. From academic resources to practical guides, the thirst for knowledge can be quenched through diverse and reputable sources.

XIX. Tools for BTU Calculations

Understanding the tools for BTU calculations is akin to having a well-equipped toolbox. Thermocouples, psychrometers, anemometers, and advanced software contribute to the precision required in HVAC design.

XX. Recap of Key Takeaways

Our journey has been a comprehensive expedition into the world of efficient cooling. From the theoretical foundations to practical applications, we've navigated through the intricacies of creating comfortable and energy-efficient residential spaces.

In closing, the knowledge gained here serves as a compass, guiding homeowners, HVAC professionals, and enthusiasts towards a future where cooling is not just a necessity but an art mastered through understanding and innovation. May your spaces remain cool, comfortable, and energy-conscious.

Empowering Readers to Make Informed e Decisions

Empowering Readers to Make Informed Decisions

In a world inundated with choices, making informed decisions becomes paramount. Nowhere is this more evident than in the realm of technology and electronics. As we navigate through an ever-evolving landscape of gadgets, devices, and digital innovations, the need for clarity and understanding is more crucial than ever.

I. Introduction

Welcome to a comprehensive guide aimed at empowering readers to navigate the complex world of electronics with confidence and insight. From the latest smartphones to cutting-edge home appliances, this journey is designed to demystify the intricacies, enabling you to make decisions that align with your needs and preferences.

II. Understanding Technological Jargon

Before diving into specific electronic devices, let's unravel the often perplexing world of technological jargon. From megapixels in cameras to gigahertz in processors, gaining clarity on these terms ensures that you can decipher product specifications with ease.

III. Choosing the Right Smartphone

Smartphones have become an integral part of our daily lives. This section provides an in-depth exploration of factors to consider when selecting a smartphone, including camera capabilities, processing power, battery life, and the often-overlooked software experience.

IV. Navigating the World of Smart Home Devices

As our homes become smarter, understanding the array of devices available is essential. From smart thermostats to connected kitchen appliances, this section delves into the functionalities and benefits of integrating these technologies into your living space.

V. Deciphering Laptop and PC Specifications

When it comes to computers, the multitude of specifications can be overwhelming. This segment breaks down key elements like processors, RAM, storage, and graphics, empowering you to choose a device that aligns with your computing needs.

VI. Ensuring Quality Audio Experiences

From headphones to home audio systems, this portion of the guide delves into the nuances of audio technology. Whether you're an audiophile or someone seeking reliable sound solutions, understanding features like driver types and frequency response is paramount.

VII. Making Sense of Wearable Technology

The world of wearables, from fitness trackers to smartwatches, is expanding rapidly. Here, we explore the functionalities that define these devices and guide you in selecting wearables that seamlessly integrate into your lifestyle.

VIII. Eco-Friendly Electronics

As environmental concerns take center stage, choosing eco-friendly electronics is a responsible decision. This chapter sheds light on energy-efficient devices, recyclable materials, and companies committed to sustainable practices.

IX. Evaluating Gaming Gadgets

For gaming enthusiasts, evaluating the latest consoles, graphics cards, and accessories is a thrilling yet challenging task. Uncover the key aspects to consider when immersing yourself in the vibrant world of gaming technology.

X. Ensuring Cybersecurity in a Connected World

With increased connectivity comes the need for heightened cybersecurity. Discover tips and strategies to protect your electronic devices from cyber threats, ensuring a secure and seamless digital experience.

XI. The Future of Electronics

Peering into the future, we explore emerging technologies set to reshape the electronic landscape. From advancements in artificial intelligence to breakthroughs in battery technology, this glimpse into the future prepares you for what lies ahead.

XII. Empowering Readers

The goal of this guide is not just to provide information but to empower you, the reader, to make decisions that resonate with your lifestyle and preferences. Each section equips you with knowledge, enabling you to navigate the electronic marketplace with confidence.

In closing, let this guide be your trusted companion as you embark on the journey of selecting, understanding, and using electronic devices. By making informed decisions, you contribute to a tech-savvy world where technology seamlessly integrates into our lives, enhancing our experiences and enriching our daily interactions. Happy reading and empowered decision-making!

Conclusion

Conclusion

In the vast landscape of electronic devices and technology, we've embarked on a journey together, unraveling complexities, exploring innovations, and empowering you, the reader, to make informed decisions. As we conclude this comprehensive guide, let's reflect on the key insights and takeaways that define the essence of our exploration.

I. Empowerment through Knowledge

Knowledge is the cornerstone of confident decision-making. By understanding the intricacies of technological jargon, deciphering specifications, and embracing the functionalities of diverse electronic devices, you've gained a robust foundation. This knowledge empowers you to navigate the dynamic world of electronics with ease and precision.

II. Tailoring Choices to Your Lifestyle

The diversity of electronic devices presented—from smartphones to smart home technologies, laptops to wearables—allows you to tailor your choices to align with your unique lifestyle. Whether you're a tech enthusiast, a fitness aficionado, or someone seeking eco-friendly options, the guide has equipped you to make choices that resonate with your preferences.

III. Navigating Complexity with Clarity

As we explored the future of electronics, delved into sustainable practices, and unraveled the nuances of gaming gadgets, you've navigated through complex realms with clarity. The guide acted as your compass, providing clear directions amidst the intricacies of evolving technologies.

IV. Securing Your Digital Experience

In an era of increased connectivity, the importance of cybersecurity cannot be overstated. The guide has not only highlighted the significance of securing your electronic devices but has also offered practical tips to ensure a safe and protected digital experience.

V. Looking Ahead

The final chapters provided a glimpse into the future of electronics, teasing upcoming advancements in AI, sustainable practices, and gaming technologies.

By staying informed about these trends, you're well-prepared to embrace the innovations that tomorrow holds.

In essence, this guide has been more than a compilation of information; it's been a companion in your quest for electronic wisdom. From the foundational concepts to the cutting-edge innovations, each word has been crafted to enlighten and empower.

As you step forward into the world of electronics, remember that your choices matter. Each device you select contributes to the technological landscape, influencing not only your experiences but also the collective trajectory of innovation.

May this guide serve as a source of reference and inspiration, fostering a community of tech-savvy individuals who embrace the potential of electronic devices while making conscious and informed decisions.

In closing, let the knowledge gained within these pages be a beacon, guiding you through the ever-evolving world of electronics. The journey doesn't end here; it extends into the future, where each new device represents a chapter in the ongoing narrative of technological advancement.

Thank you for joining us on this expedition through the realm of electronics. May your choices be wise, your devices be innovative, and your experiences be nothing short of extraordinary.

Happy exploring and empowered decision-making!

| Page

www.ingramcontent.com/pod-product-compliance
Lightning Source LLC
Chambersburg PA
CBHW070712250726
48662CB00001B/375